"9Marks, as a ministry, has taken basic biblical teachin the hands of pastors. Bobby, by way of these study gu delivered it to the person in the pew. I am unaware of ι and practically helps Christians understand God's plan for the local church. I can't wait to use these studies in my own congregation."

   Jeramie Rinne, Senior Pastor, South Shore Baptist Church, Hingham, Massachusetts

"Bobby Jamieson has done local church pastors an incredible service by writing these study guides. Clear, biblical, and practical, they introduce the biblical basis for a healthy church. But more importantly, they challenge and equip church members to be part of the process of improving their own church's health. The studies work for individual, small group, and larger group settings. I have used them for the last year at my own church and appreciate how easy they are to adapt to my own setting. I don't know of anything else like them. Highly recommended!"

   Michael Lawrence, Senior Pastor, Hinson Baptist Church, *Biblical Theology in the Life of the Church*

"This is a Bible study that is actually rooted in the Bible and involves actual study. In the 9Marks Healthy Church Study Guides series a new standard has been set for personal theological discovery and corresponding personal application. Rich exposition, compelling questions, and clear syntheses combine to give a guided tour of ecclesiology—the theology of the church. I know of no better curriculum for generating understanding of and involvement in the church than this. It will be a welcome resource in our church for years to come."

   Rick Holland, Senior Pastor, Mission Road Bible Church, Prairie Village, Kansas

"In America today we have the largest churches in the history of our nation, but the least amount of impact for Christ's kingdom. Slick marketing and finely polished vision statements are a foundation of sand. The 9Marks Healthy Church Study Guides series is a refreshing departure from church-growth materials, towards an in-depth study of God's Word that will equip God's people with his vision for his Church. These study guides will lead local congregations to abandon secular methodologies for church growth and instead rely on Christ's principles for developing healthy, God-honoring assemblies."

   Carl J. Broggi, Senior Pastor, Community Bible Church, Beaufort, South Carolina; President, Search the Scriptures Radio Ministry

"Anyone who loves Jesus will love what Jesus loves. The Bible clearly teaches that Jesus loves the church. He knows about and cares for individual churches and wants them to be spiritually healthy and vibrant. Not only has Jesus laid down his life for the church but he has also given many instructions in his Word regarding how churches are to live and function in the world. This series of Bible studies by 9Marks shows how Scripture teaches these things. Any Christian who works through this curriculum, preferably with other believers, will be helped to see in fresh ways the wisdom, love, and power of God in establishing the church on earth. These studies are biblical, practical, and accessible. I highly recommend this curriculum as a useful tool that will help any church embrace its calling to display the glory of God to a watching world."

   Thomas Ascol, Senior Pastor, Grace Baptist Church of Cape Coral, Florida; Executive Director, Founders Ministries

9MARKS HEALTHY CHURCH STUDY GUIDES

Built upon the Rock: The Church

Hearing God's Word: Expositional Preaching

The Whole Truth about God: Biblical Theology

God's Good News: The Gospel

Real Change: Conversion

Reaching the Lost: Evangelism

Committing to One Another: Church Membership

Guarding One Another: Church Discipline

Growing One Another: Discipleship in the Church

Leading One Another: Church Leadership

LEADING ONE ANOTHER: CHURCH LEADERSHIP

Bobby Jamieson
Mark Dever, General Editor
Jonathan Leeman, Managing Editor

HEALTHY CHURCH STUDY GUIDES

 CROSSWAY

WHEATON, ILLINOIS

Leading One Another: Church Leadership

Copyright © 2012 by 9Marks

Published by Crossway
      1300 Crescent Street
      Wheaton, Illinois 60187

Cover design: Dual Identity inc.

First printing 2012

Printed in the United States of America

Trade paperback ISBN: 978-1-4335-2560-5

PDF ISBN: 978-1-4335-2561-2

Mobipocket ISBN: 978-1-4335-2562-9

ePub ISBN: 978-1-4335-2563-6

Crossway is a publishing ministry of Good News Publishers.

LB		20	19	18	17	16	15	14	13	12
15	14	13	12	11	10	9	8	7	6	5	4	3	2	1

CONTENTS

INTRODUCTION

What does the local church mean to you?

Maybe you love your church. You love the people. You love the preaching, the singing. You can't wait to show up on Sunday, and you cherish fellowship with other church members throughout the week.

Maybe the church is just a place you show up to a couple times a month. You sneak in late, duck out early.

We at 9Marks are convinced that the local church is God's plan for displaying his glory to the nations. And we want to help you catch and live out that vision, together with your whole church.

The 9Marks Healthy Church Study Guides are a series of six- or seven-week studies on each of the "nine marks of a healthy church" plus one introductory study. These nine marks are the core convictions of our ministry. To provide a quick introduction to them, we've included a chapter from Mark Dever's book *What Is a Healthy Church?* with each study. We don't claim that these nine marks are the most important things about the church or the only important things about the church. But we do believe that they are biblical and therefore are helpful for churches.

So, in these studies, we're going to work through the biblical foundations and practical applications of each one. The ten studies are:

- *Built upon the Rock: The Church* (the introductory study)
- *Hearing God's Word: Expositional Preaching*
- *The Whole Truth about God: Biblical Theology*
- *God's Good News: The Gospel*
- *Real Change: Conversion*
- *Reaching the Lost: Evangelism*
- *Committing to One Another: Church Membership*

- *Guarding One Another: Church Discipline*
- *Growing One Another: Discipleship in the Church*
- *Leading One Another: Church Leadership*

Each session of these studies takes a close look at one or more passages of Scripture and considers how it applies to the life of the whole church. So, we hope that these studies are equally appropriate for Sunday school, small groups, and other contexts where a group of anywhere from two to two-hundred people can come together and discuss God's Word.

These studies are mainly driven by observation, interpretation, and application questions, so get ready to speak up! We also hope that these studies provide opportunities for people to reflect together on their experiences in the church, whatever those experiences may be.

Leaders can make life much better or much worse, can't they? Think of loving parents who make countless sacrifices for their children's good, a gifted teacher who not only instructs but also inspires, a wise head of state who pursues justice and peace, a pastor who faithfully teaches, preaches, counsels, and cares for his people.

On the other hand, we are all too familiar with abusive or irresponsible parents, teachers who are lazy or uncaring, oppressive military dictators, and pastors who spout heresy and fleece their flocks.

In view of these abuses, the first session in this study answers the question, is authority bad? Next, we take a look at God's revelation of himself as the Shepherd of his people and how God calls his people's leaders to image him. The remaining sessions in the study consider individuals who have special responsibilities within the church: elders, deacons, and you.

Because it can be abused, leadership is a risky business for those in it and those under it. But God has good plans for leadership within the church. Let's explore those plans together and ask God to bless our churches with leaders—shepherds, in fact—after his own heart.

AN IMPORTANT MARK OF A HEALTHY CHURCH: BIBLICAL CHURCH LEADERSHIP

BY MARK DEVER

(Originally published as chapter 13 of What Is a Healthy Church?*)*

What kind of leadership does a healthy church have? Is it a congregation that strives to ensure that the gospel is faithfully preached? Yes (Galatians 1). Is it deacons who model service in the affairs of the church? Yes (Acts 6). Is it a pastor who is faithful in preaching the Word of God? Yes (2 Timothy 4). But the Bible presents one more leadership gift to churches to help them become healthy: the position of elder.

Surely there are many useful things we could say about church leadership from the Bible; yet I want to focus primarily on this question of elders, since I fear a lot of churches don't know what they're missing. As a pastor, I pray that Christ will place within our fellowships men whose spiritual gifts and pastoral concern indicate that God has called them to be elders. May he prepare many such men!

If God has so gifted a certain man in the church with exemplary character, pastoral wisdom, and gifts of teaching, and if, after prayer, the church recognizes these things, then he should be set apart as an elder.

WHAT IS AN ELDER?

In Acts 6, the young church in Jerusalem began to bicker over how food was being distributed to widows. The apostles therefore called upon the church to select several men who could better oversee this distribution. The apostles chose to delegate this particular task so that they could then "give [their] attention to prayer and the ministry of the word" (Acts 6:4 NIV).

That, in the briefest terms, appears to be the division of labor between elders and deacons that the rest of the New Testament develops. Elders are especially devoted to prayer and the ministry of the Word for the church, while deacons help to sustain the church's physical operations.

Are you beginning to see what a gift this is to you, churches? God is essentially saying, "I'm going to take several men from among you and set them aside to pray for you and to teach you about me."

ELDERS AND CONGREGATIONS

All churches have had individuals designated to perform the functions of elders, even if those individuals are called by other titles, such as deacon or director. The three New Testament titles for this office, which are used interchangeably, are *episkopos* (overseer or bishop), *presbuteros* (elder), and *poimain* (shepherd or pastor). All three are used for the same men, for instance, in Acts 20:17 and 20:28.

When evangelicals hear the word *elder*, however, many of them immediately think "Presbyterian." Yet the first Congregationalists (capital C, pointing to a formal group of churches) back in the sixteenth century taught that eldership was an office for New Testament churches. Elders could also be found in Baptist churches in America throughout the eighteenth and into the nineteenth centuries. In fact, the first president of the Southern Baptist Convention, W. B. Johnson, wrote a treatise in 1846 calling Baptist churches to use a plurality of elders since the practice was biblical.

Baptists and Presbyterians do disagree in two areas concerning elders (and I think the issues at play here are relevant to those who are not Baptist or Presbyterian). First and most fundamentally, we who are Baptists are congregationalists (lowercase c, referring to a practice). We believe that the Bible teaches that the final decision on matters rests with the congregation as a whole, not with a church's elders or anyone outside the church body. When Jesus was teaching his disciples about confronting a sinful brother, he said that the congregation was the final court of appeal—not the elders, not a bishop or pope, not a council or convention (Matt. 18:17). When the apostles sought out several men to act as deacons, as we just discussed, they gave the decision over to the congregation.

In Paul's letters, too, the congregation appears to assume final responsibility. In 1 Corinthians 5, Paul blames not the pastor, elders, or deacons for tolerating a man's sin, but the congregation. In 2 Corinthians 2, Paul refers to what a majority of them had done in disciplining an erring member. In Galatians 1, Paul calls on the congregations themselves to judge the false teaching they had been hearing. In 2 Timothy 4, Paul reproves not just the false teachers but also those who paid them to teach what their itching ears wanted to hear. Elders lead, but they do so, biblically and necessarily, within the bounds recognized by the congregation. In that sense, elders and every other board or committee in a Baptist church act in what is finally an advisory capacity to the whole congregation.

Second, Baptists and Presbyterians have disagreed over the roles and responsibilities of elders, largely due to different understandings of the following words written by Paul for Timothy: "The elders who direct the affairs of the church well are worthy of double honor, especially those whose work is preaching and teaching" (1 Tim. 5:17 NIV). Presbyterians understand this verse to be establishing two classes of elders—ruling elders and teaching elders. Baptists don't recognize this formal division but understand the verse to suggest that certain individuals among a group of elders will simply be given more fully, as a practical matter, to preaching and teaching. After all, Paul clearly tells Timothy earlier in the letter that a basic qualification of every elder is that he is "able to teach" (1 Tim. 3:2; see also Titus 1:9). Baptists, therefore, have often denied the appropriateness of appointing elders who are not capable of teaching Scripture.

PLURALITY OF ELDERS

Where Baptists and Presbyterians often agreed in the eighteenth century was that there should be a plurality (or multiple number) of elders in each local church. The New Testament never suggests a specific number of elders for a particular congregation, but it clearly and consistently refers to the "elders" of a local church in the plural (for example, Acts 14:23; 16:4; 20:17; 21:18; Titus 1:5; James 5:14).

Today, not only are more and more Baptist churches rediscovering this, but also churches from many other denominations, as well as independent churches, are increasingly recognizing this basic biblical idea.

A plurality of elders does not mean that the pastor has no distinctive role. There are many references in the New Testament to preaching and preachers that would not apply to all the elders in a congregation. In Corinth, for instance, Paul gave himself exclusively to preaching in a way that lay elders in a church could not (Acts 18:5; 1 Cor. 9:14; 1 Tim. 4:13; 5:17). Also, preachers seemed to relocate to an area for the express purpose of preaching (Rom. 10:14–15), whereas elders seemed settled among the community (Titus 1:5).

As the regular voice that proclaims God's Word, a faithful preacher will probably find that a congregation and the other elders treat him as the first among equals and "especially" worthy of double honor (1 Tim. 5:17). Still, the preacher or pastor is, fundamentally, just one more elder, formally equal with every other man called by the congregation to act in this capacity.

BENEFITS OF ELDERS

My own experience as a pastor has confirmed the usefulness of following the New Testament practice of sharing, wherever possible, the responsibility for pastoring a local church with other men rooted in the congregation.

Decisions involving the church but not requiring the attention of all the members should fall not to the pastor alone, but to the elders as a whole. This is sometimes cumbersome, but it has immense benefits. It rounds out the pastor's gifts, making up for some of his defects and supplementing his judgment. It creates support in the congregation for decisions, helping unity and leaving leaders less exposed to unjust criticism. It makes leadership more rooted and permanent and allows for more mature continuity. It encourages the church to take more responsibility for its spirituality and helps make the church less dependent on its employees.

This practice of a plurality of elders is unusual among Baptist churches today, but there is a growing trend toward it among Baptists and many others—and for good reason. It was needed in New Testament churches and it is needed now.

WHAT ABOUT DEACONS?

Many modern churches tend to confuse elders with either the church staff or the deacons. Deacons also fill a New Testament office, one rooted in Acts 6, as we saw. While any absolute distinction between the two offices is difficult, deacons are generally concerned with the practical details of church life: administration, maintenance, and the care of church members with physical needs. In many churches today, the deacons have either taken over the role of spiritual oversight or they have left it entirely in the hands of one man, the pastor. It would benefit churches to again distinguish the roles of elders and deacons. Do churches not need both types of servants?

SHOULDERING THE BURDEN AND PRIVILEGE

Eldership is the biblical office that I hold as a pastor—I am the main preaching elder. But I work together with a group of elders for the edification of the church. Some are on staff, but the majority are not. We meet regularly to pray, to talk, and to form recommendations for the deacons or the whole church. It's difficult to put into words how much these men have loved both me and our entire congregation by sharing the burden—and privilege—of pastoring. I thank God regularly for these fellow workers.

Clearly, eldership is a biblical idea that has practical value. If implemented in our churches, it could help pastors immensely by removing weight from their shoulders and even removing their own petty tyrannies from their churches. Furthermore, the character qualities listed by Paul for eldership, aside from the ability to teach, are qualities every Christian should work toward (1 Timothy 3; Titus 1). Publicly affirming certain individuals as exemplary, then, helps to present a model for other Christians, especially Christian men. Indeed, the practice of recognizing godly, discerning, trusted laymen as elders is another mark of a healthy church.

WEEK 1
IS AUTHORITY BAD?

GETTING STARTED

1. What kind of authority relationships are you in? Whose authority are you under? Do you exercise authority over anyone?

2. What are some experiences with authority you've had that stand out to you? Were they good, bad, or ugly?

Many people in our culture are highly suspicious of authority. After all, it can be used to oppress, abuse, and denigrate people. The fact that authority is so often abused has led some people to regard authority itself as inherently evil. But, as we'll see from Scripture in this study, authority itself is a good gift from God that images his rule over us.

MAIN IDEA

Authority is a good gift from God that images his rule over us.

DIGGING IN

In Daniel 4, God sends Nebuchadnezzar, the king of Babylon, out into the wilderness. God throws him down from his high place and causes him to live as a wild beast, so that he would know who was truly in charge in the universe. Here's what Nebuchadnezzar says at the end of that period:

> [34] At the end of the days I, Nebuchadnezzar, lifted my eyes to heaven, and my reason returned to me, and I blessed the Most High, and praised and honored him who lives forever,
>
> > for his dominion is an everlasting dominion,
> > and his kingdom endures from generation to generation;

³⁵ all the inhabitants of the earth are accounted as nothing,
    and he does according to his will among the host of heaven
    and among the inhabitants of the earth;
and none can stay his hand
    or say to him, "What have you done?" (Dan. 4:34–35)

1. What does Nebuchadnezzar confess about God's dominion and kingdom in this passage?

2. What does Nebuchadnezzar say about God's relationship to people? How would you describe that relationship?

3. How does your heart react to this kind of language, to the idea that God rules over everything and does all that he pleases in heaven and on earth?

In Genesis 1, we read about how God created the whole universe, including the earth and humankind. Here's what God said when he created humans:

²⁶ Then God said, "Let us make man in our image, after our likeness. And let them have dominion over the fish of the sea and over the birds of the heavens and over the livestock and over all the earth and over every creeping thing that creeps on the earth."

    ²⁷ So God created man in his own image,
        in the image of God he created him;
        male and female he created them.

    ²⁸ And God blessed them. And God said to them, "Be fruitful and multiply and fill the earth and subdue it and have dominion over the fish of the sea and over the birds of the heavens and over every living thing that moves on the earth." (Gen. 1:26–28)

4. In whose image is man created (v. 26)?

5. What does the fact of being made in the image of God mean for man's relationship to creation (vv. 26, 28)?

6. What do we learn about authority from this passage?

7. In a number of different places in Scripture, God gives special kinds of authority to specific groups of people. Read each of the following passages:

- Romans 13:1–7
- Ephesians 6:1–4
- Hebrews 13:7, 17

Answer the following questions about each passage:

- To whom does God grant authority?
- What does he grant them authority to do?
- What response does God require from those who are under this authority?

King David had more experience with authority than most people in the Bible. He knew what good came when authority was used wisely, and he knew by sad experience what happened when people abused authority—because he did so himself (2 Sam. 11–12). It should arrest our attention, then, that David's last words, which are recorded for us in 2 Samuel 23, are about authority:

> ¹ Now these are the last words of David:
> The oracle of David, the son of Jesse,
>   the oracle of the man who was raised on high,
> the anointed of the God of Jacob,
>   the sweet psalmist of Israel:
> ² "The Spirit of the LORD speaks by me;
>   his word is on my tongue.
> ³ The God of Israel has spoken;
>   the Rock of Israel has said to me:
> When one rules justly over men,
>   ruling in the fear of God,
> ⁴ he dawns on them like the morning light,
>   like the sun shining forth on a cloudless morning,
>   like rain that makes grass to sprout from the earth." (vv. 1–4)

8. What characterizes the exercise of authority that David describes in verse 3?

9. Why is it important for kings, and all those who exercise authority, to wield their authority "in the fear of God" (v. 3)? What will happen if they don't?

10. According to David, what happens when a king rules justly and in the fear of God? Have you ever experienced fruit like this in your own life from the godly exercise of authority?

11. In light of all of these passages, how would you respond to someone who thought that authority itself is a bad thing?

12. List out all the authorities you are under and all the ways you exercise authority over others. What does it practically look like for you to live under authority and exercise authority in a godly way? Consider passages such as:

- Ephesians 5:22–33
- Ephesians 6:1–4
- Ephesians 6:5–9
- 1 Peter 2:13–17
- 1 Peter 2:18–25

WEEK 2
GOD, THE SHEPHERD OF HIS PEOPLE

GETTING STARTED

1. What are some common names, titles, images, and metaphors for leaders? What does each of these convey about the nature of leadership?

MAIN IDEA

Throughout Scripture, God reveals himself to be the Shepherd of his people. From God's revelation of himself as Shepherd, we learn of his compassion, tenderness, faithfulness, justice, and loving care for every single one of his people.

DIGGING IN

It will be important to work through this lesson with an open Bible at the ready, since we'll be studying a long portion of Scripture.

Ezekiel 34 is a sweeping passage. In it, God condemns the wickedness of the shepherds of Israel, reveals his own character as the shepherd of his people, and promises to deliver his people in the future.

1. Read Ezekiel 34:1–24. What have the shepherds of Israel done? What have they not done (vv. 1–4)? What are some of the concrete events this metaphorical language is likely referring to? (See also vv. 18–19.)

2. What has happened to the people of Israel as a result (vv. 5–6)?

3. What is God's attitude toward the shepherds? What is he going to do to them (vv. 7–10)?

4. *What are all the different things God promises to do for his sheep (vv. 11–16)? List them below.*

5. *What does God's promise to gather and feed his sheep reveal about his character (vv. 11–14)?*

6. *What does God's promise to seek the lost, bring back the strayed, and strengthen the weak reveal about his character (vv. 15–16)?*

7. *What does God's promise to destroy the fat and the strong (who have made themselves so by abusing others, vv. 1–6) and to feed his sheep in justice reveal about his character (v. 16)?*

8. *What does God's revelation of himself as the shepherd of his people teach us about how we should relate to him? (For rich food for thought, read Psalm 23! See also Psalm 95:6–7.)*

9. *Whom does God promise to set up over his flock when he rescues them (vv. 22–24)?*

10. *How does God fulfill this promise? (Hint: See Jeremiah 23:5–6; Luke 1:32–33; and John 10:11–18.)*

11. *In Jeremiah 3:14, God promises to gather his people to Israel again, just as he promises in Ezekiel 34. But then in verse 15 we see another facet of God's redemptive plan:*

> And I will give you shepherds after my own heart, who will feed you with knowledge and understanding. (Jer. 3:15)

What does this prophecy add to our understanding of how God will shepherd his people? How is this prophecy fulfilled? (Hint: See Ephesians 4:8–12.)

You may be surprised to learn that the word our English Bibles render *pastor* is actually "shepherd" in Greek. So, when we read about pastors in the Bible, we should think about shepherds. That's why Peter writes to the elders of local churches,

[1] So I exhort the elders among you, as a fellow elder and a witness of the sufferings of Christ, as well as a partaker in the glory that is going to be revealed: [2] shepherd the flock of God that is among you, exercising oversight, not under compulsion, but willingly, as God would have you; not for shameful gain, but eagerly; [3] not domineering over those in your charge, but being examples to the flock. [4] And when the chief Shepherd appears, you will receive the unfading crown of glory. (1 Pet. 5:1–4)

In Ezekiel 34 we see God's own character as the shepherd of his people, and we read of his promise to personally shepherd his people through the Son of David. In Jeremiah 3:15, God promises to send his people shepherds after his own heart. And in 1 Peter 5, almost as if he's got Ezekiel 34 open right in front of him, Peter charges pastors to shepherd God's flock as God would have them.

12. What do all these passages, taken together, teach about pastors' job descriptions and about how they should exercise their ministry?

13. What do these passages have to say to the person who is skeptical or uneasy about authority in the church? How do these passages confront, comfort, and encourage such an individual?

14. Can you give an example of a leader who you have witnessed shepherding others in way that looks something like the divine Shepherd?

WEEK 3
ELDERS: MINISTERS OF THE WORD AND SHEPHERDS OF THE CHURCH

GETTING STARTED

1. What do churches typically expect their pastors to do? List everything you can think of.

2. Do you think there's anything churches typically expect pastors to do that they shouldn't? Or anything that churches don't expect but they should?

MAIN IDEA

Elders are called to lead the church by teaching God's Word, shepherding the flock one by one, and serving as examples of godly character.

DIGGING IN

In the New Testament, the church's spiritual leaders are interchangeably referred to as elders, overseers, or pastors (see, for example, Acts 20:17, 28; Titus 1:5, 7). Since "elder" is the most common title, that's the one we'll use.

In this study, we're going to look at what elders are supposed to do. In the next study, we'll think about the qualifications for being an elder. As with the previous study, it will be good to go through this with an open Bible.

In 1 Peter 5, Peter directly addresses local church elders, saying,

[1] So I exhort the elders among you, as a fellow elder and a witness of the sufferings of Christ, as well as a partaker in the glory that is going to be revealed: [2] shepherd the flock of God that is among you, exer-

cising oversight, not under compulsion, but willingly, as God would have you; not for shameful gain, but eagerly; [3] not domineering over those in your charge, but being examples to the flock. [4] And when the chief Shepherd appears, you will receive the unfading crown of glory. [5] Likewise, you who are younger, be subject to the elders. Clothe yourselves, all of you, with humility toward one another, for "God opposes the proud but gives grace to the humble." (5:1–5)

1. On what basis does Peter appeal to the elders (v. 1)? Why do you think he mentions these things before exhorting the elders?

2. What is the main command Peter gives to the elders (v. 2)?

3. What does it mean, practically, to shepherd a church? What are some examples of what shepherding entails?

4. In verses 2 and 3, Peter alternates between telling the elders how they should and shouldn't shepherd the flock. Fill in the chart below in order to map out what Peter is saying, and then discuss:

Don't Shepherd Like This . . .	Instead, Shepherd Like *This* . . .

- What strikes you about what Peter says *not* to do? Why do you think he prohibits these things?
- Does anything strike you about what Peter says to do?
- What kind of fruit do you think would come from a ministry in which the elders faithfully obeyed these instructions?

5. What does Peter say will happen for faithful elders when Jesus comes back (v. 4)? Why should this encourage elders? Why should it humble them?

6. What does Peter tell the rest of the church to do in response to the elders' ministry (v. 5)? Why does this require humility on our part?

In Acts 20, Paul gathers the elders of the church in Ephesus together as he passes through town on his way to Jerusalem in order to instruct them about how to carry out their ministry. We read,

[17] Now from Miletus he sent to Ephesus and called the elders of the church to come to him. [18] And when they came to him, he said to them:

"You yourselves know how I lived among you the whole time from the first day that I set foot in Asia, [19] serving the Lord with all humility and with tears and with trials that happened to me through the plots of the Jews; [20] how I did not shrink from declaring to you anything that was profitable, and teaching you in public and from house to house, [21] testifying both to Jews and to Greeks of repentance toward God and of faith in our Lord Jesus Christ. [22] And now, behold, I am going to Jerusalem, constrained by the Spirit, not knowing what will happen to me there, [23] except that the Holy Spirit testifies to me in every city that imprisonment and afflictions await me. [24] But I do not account my life of any value nor as precious to myself, if only I may finish my course and the ministry that I received from the Lord Jesus, to testify to the gospel of the grace of God. [25] And now, behold, I know that none of you among whom I have gone about proclaiming the kingdom will see my face again. [26] Therefore I testify to you this day that I am innocent of the blood of all, [27] for I did not shrink from declaring to you the whole counsel of God. [28] Pay careful attention to yourselves and to all the flock, in which the Holy Spirit has made you overseers, to care for the church of God, which he obtained with his own blood. [29] I know that after my departure fierce wolves will come in among you, not sparing the flock; [30] and from among your own selves will arise men speaking twisted things, to draw away the disciples after them. [31] Therefore be alert, remembering that for three years I did not cease night or day to admonish everyone with tears. [32] And now I commend you to God and to the word of his grace, which is able to build you up and to give you the inheritance among all those who are sanctified. [33] I coveted no one's silver or gold or apparel. [34] You yourselves know that these hands ministered to my necessities and to those who were with me. [35] In all things I have shown you that by working hard in this way we must help the weak and remember the words of the Lord Jesus, how he himself said, 'It is more blessed to give than to receive.'"

[36] And when he had said these things, he knelt down and prayed with them all. [37] And there was much weeping on the part of all;

they embraced Paul and kissed him, [38] being sorrowful most of all because of the word he had spoken, that they would not see his face again. And they accompanied him to the ship.

7. *Why does Paul so extensively discuss his own way of life and teaching in this address to the Ephesian elders? What is he doing?*

8. *What characterized Paul's way of life among the Ephesians (vv. 18–21, 27, 31, 33–35)?*

9. *How does Paul's life hold up to Peter's teaching about how elders should live and exercise their ministries? (Hint: Look for explicit points of comparison between the two; there are lots!)*

10. *What does Paul charge the Ephesian elders to do? List all of his directions for them below. (See especially verses 28, 31, and 35.)*

11. *Looking over these two passages, do you think elders have an easy job? Why or why not?*

12. *Hebrews 13:17 says, "Obey your leaders and submit to them, for they are keeping watch over your souls, as those who will have to give an account. Let them do this with joy and not with groaning, for that would be of no advantage to you." Given all that elders are responsible to do, what are some ways that you can help ensure that they shepherd you with joy and not with groaning?*

13. *What are some specific ways you can pray for your pastors or elders this week that are based on these passages? Write a few out below and then discuss them. Will you commit to praying these things for your elders, not only this week, but also on a regular basis?*

WEEK 4
FINDING THE RIGHT MEN: QUALIFICATIONS FOR ELDERS

GETTING STARTED

1. What kinds of things qualify people for leadership in business? What about in local communities? In the government?

2. What do you think qualifies someone for spiritual leadership in the church?

MAIN IDEA

Elders must be men of consistently exemplary Christian character, must lead their families well, and must be able to teach God's Word.

DIGGING IN

In 1 Timothy 3:1–7, Paul lays out qualifications for elders. He writes,

> [1] The saying is trustworthy: If anyone aspires to the office of overseer, he desires a noble task. [2] Therefore an overseer must be above reproach, the husband of one wife, sober-minded, self-controlled, respectable, hospitable, able to teach, [3] not a drunkard, not violent but gentle, not quarrelsome, not a lover of money. [4] He must manage his own household well, with all dignity keeping his children submissive, [5] for if someone does not know how to manage his own household, how will he care for God's church? [6] He must not be a recent convert, or he may become puffed up with conceit and fall into the condemnation of the devil. [7] Moreover, he must be well thought of by outsiders, so that he may not fall into disgrace, into a snare of the devil.

Note: In this passage, Paul describes the office of elder using the term *episkopos*, which means "overseer." Throughout the New Testament, the terms "elder" and "overseer" refer to the same office. (See, for example, the nearly identical list of qualifications in Titus 1:5–9, as well as Acts 20:17, 28; Philippians 1:1; 1 Timothy 5:17–19; and 1 Peter 5:1–4.)

1. In this passage, Paul presents a series of qualifications for men who desire to be elders. List them all below.

1)

2)

3)

4)

5)

6)

7)

8)

9)

10)

11)

12)

13)

14)

2. What does it mean to be "above reproach" (v. 2)?

3. The Greek phrase translated "husband of one wife" could also be translated as "one-woman man" (v. 2). What does this qualification require of married men?

4. The words "sober-minded," "self-controlled," and "respectable" all refer to similar qualities (v. 2). List some concrete examples of what they look like in action.

5. Why do you think hospitality is a qualification for an elder (v. 2)? What should Christian hospitality consist of?

New Testament scholar D. A. Carson has observed that perhaps the most extraordinary thing about the biblical qualifications for elders is that they are not all that extraordinary. In fact, almost all of them are required of all Christians elsewhere in the New Testament (see Matt. 5:27–30; Rom. 12:13; Eph. 6:4; 1 Thess. 4:12; Titus 2:1–12; 1 Pet. 1:13). Apart from not being a new convert, the one qualification that is not required of all Christians elsewhere is that elders must be "able to teach" (1 Tim. 3:2).

6. Read Titus 1:9–10. Why is it important that elders be able to teach, as verse 2 says?

7. Read 1 Timothy 2:11–15. Given that all elders are required to be able to teach and that teaching the church is one of their main responsibilities (Titus 1:9–10), does Scripture allow women to be elders?

8. What do all of the qualifications listed in verse 3 ("not a drunkard, not violent but gentle, not quarrelsome, not a lover of money") have in common?

9. Why does Paul insist that a man must manage his household well in order to be an elder (vv. 4–5)?

10. Why would a recent convert be susceptible to becoming puffed up with conceit and falling into the condemnation of the Devil (v. 6)?

11. In verse 7 Paul insists that an elder must be well thought of by outsiders. What is at stake in an elder's reputation among non-Christians?

12. In verses 6 and 7, Paul twice warns against elders falling into Satan's traps. In what ways are elders particularly susceptible to temptation?

13. How can this list of qualifications guide your prayers for your church's leaders? List several specific examples.

14. What are some practical ways you can encourage these qualities in other church members? What are some ways you can cultivate these qualities yourself? After all, elders are required to meet these standards so as to serve as examples for the whole church to imitate (see 1 Pet. 5:3).

WEEK 5
DEACONS: SERVANTS OF
THE CHURCH

GETTING STARTED

1. When practical needs arise in your church, who tends to take care of them?

2. What are some of the practical needs that arise in your church? What challenges can they pose to:

- The unity of the church?
- The church's leaders?

MAIN IDEA

Deacons are to serve the church by caring for its practical needs and freeing up the elders to devote themselves to the ministry of the Word and prayer.

DIGGING IN

What we see in Acts 6:1–7 is likely the historical roots of the office of deacon. It begins with a tense conflict:

> [1] Now in these days when the disciples were increasing in number, a complaint by the Hellenists arose against the Hebrews because their widows were being neglected in the daily distribution. [2] And the twelve summoned the full number of the disciples and said, "It is not right that we should give up preaching the word of God to serve tables. [3] Therefore, brothers, pick out from among you seven men of good repute, full of the Spirit and of wisdom, whom we will appoint to this duty. [4] But we will devote ourselves to prayer and to the ministry of the word." [5] And what they said pleased the whole gathering, and they chose Stephen, a man full of faith and of the Holy Spirit,

and Philip, and Prochorus, and Nicanor, and Timon, and Parmenas, and Nicolaus, a proselyte of Antioch. ⁶ These they set before the apostles, and they prayed and laid their hands on them.

⁷ And the word of God continued to increase, and the number of the disciples multiplied greatly in Jerusalem, and a great many of the priests became obedient to the faith. (6:1–7)

1. What problem did the church in Jerusalem face in this passage (v. 1)?

2. What was the apostles' solution to the problem (vv. 2–4)?

3. What kind of men did the apostles tell the congregation to pick out for this task (v. 3)?

4. What rationale did the apostles give for why they delegated this task to another group of people (v. 4)?

The Greek word from which we get the term "deacon" is *diakonos*, which means servant. It was used to describe many different kinds of work, including waiting tables (the related verb is used in 6:2). And the apostles resolved to devote themselves to the *diakonia*, the ministry, of the Word and prayer (6:4). Thus, while this passage doesn't use the term "deacon" to describe the men who handled the distribution of food, it seems likely that Luke is recording this incident to describe the historical origins of what later became the office of deacon.

By the time the apostle Paul wrote 1 Timothy, the office of deacon was apparently well established in many churches (see Phil. 1:1). Thus, in 1 Timothy 3, after listing the qualifications for elders, Paul lays out the qualifications for deacons as well:

⁸ Deacons likewise must be dignified, not double-tongued, not addicted to much wine, not greedy for dishonest gain. ⁹ They must hold the mystery of the faith with a clear conscience. ¹⁰ And let them also be tested first; then let them serve as deacons if they prove themselves blameless. ¹¹ Their wives [or "deaconesses"] likewise must be dignified, not slanderers, but sober-minded, faithful in all

things. ¹² Let deacons each be the husband of one wife, managing their children and their own households well. ¹³ For those who serve well as deacons gain a good standing for themselves and also great confidence in the faith that is in Christ Jesus. (3:8–13)

5. In verse 8, Paul lists several qualifications for deacons that pertain to character. List these qualifications below and then try to find a word or phrase that summarizes them. What overall picture do these qualifications paint?

6. What does it mean to "hold the mystery of the faith with a clear conscience" (v. 9)?

7. Why do you think Paul insists that deacons be tested before they serve (v. 10)? (For a similar line of thought, see Paul's instruction that an elder must not be a recent convert in verse 6.)

8. What does Paul require of deacons in terms of family life (v. 12)?

9. Read 1 Timothy 3:4–5. What's present in this qualification for elders that's absent in the qualification for deacons in 3:12? What do you think this teaches us about the difference between the two offices?

10. What do deacons who serve well gain (v. 13)? Why do you think this is?

11. Are there any qualifications for elders that aren't qualifications for deacons? What does that tell us about the difference between elders' and deacons' responsibilities?

At the beginning of the lesson we suggested that Acts 6 gives historical background to the office of deacon but does not describe the founding of the office itself. (Note that the term "deacon" isn't used in the passage.) If that's the case, then the office of deacon is only mentioned two or maybe three times in the New Testament (Phil. 1:1; 1 Tim. 3:8–13; possibly Rom. 16:1).

Based on what little information Scripture gives us, it seems that the role of deacons is to care for the church's practical needs in order to enable the elders to focus on the ministry of the Word and prayer, as the apostles did (Acts 6:4). That's why deacons are required to be people of godly character, integrity, and proven faith, yet they are not required to be able to teach, and they are not said to shepherd or lead the church the way the elders are.

12. Within that basic framework, what are some more specific ways you think deacons should serve in the church? What are some needs in your church that deacons could address?

13. What are some challenges deacons face? What are some ways you can encourage and pray for your church's deacons in light of these challenges?

WEEK 6
YOUR RESPONSIBILITY FOR
THE CHURCH

GETTING STARTED

1. What are some things (or people!) in your life that you're responsible for?

2. How do those responsibilities impact your day-to-day life, priorities, and decisions?

MAIN IDEA

While elders have a special responsibility to preach the Word and shepherd the church, the whole congregation is finally accountable before God for the church's doctrine and discipline.

DIGGING IN

Galatians 1 is one of the most heated passages in all of Paul's letters. He writes,

> ¹ Paul, an apostle—not from men nor through man, but through Jesus Christ and God the Father, who raised him from the dead—² and all the brothers who are with me,
>
> To the churches of Galatia:
>
> ³ Grace to you and peace from God our Father and the Lord Jesus Christ, ⁴ who gave himself for our sins to deliver us from the present evil age, according to the will of our God and Father, ⁵ to whom be the glory forever and ever. Amen.
>
> ⁶ I am astonished that you are so quickly deserting him who called you in the grace of Christ and are turning to a different gospel—⁷ not that there is another one, but there are some who trouble you and want to distort the gospel of Christ. ⁸ But even if we or an angel from heaven should preach to you a gospel contrary to the one we preached to you, let him be accursed. ⁹ As we have said before, so

now I say again: If anyone is preaching to you a gospel contrary to the one you received, let him be accursed. [10] For am I now seeking the approval of man, or of God? Or am I trying to please man? If I were still trying to please man, I would not be a servant of Christ. (1:1–10)

1. What is Paul astonished about (vv. 6–7)?

2. What are those who are troubling the Galatians doing (v. 7)?

3. On whom does Paul pronounce a curse (twice!) in verses 8 and 9? Why is preaching a false gospel such a serious matter?

4. Who is Paul's letter addressed to? Is he only speaking to the churches' leaders?

5. According to this passage, who is ultimately responsible for ensuring that the church is teaching sound doctrine?

In 1 Corinthians 5, Paul addresses another serious issue that arose in a local church, except this time the issue wasn't doctrinal, it was moral. Paul writes,

[1] It is actually reported that there is sexual immorality among you, and of a kind that is not tolerated even among pagans, for a man has his father's wife. [2] And you are arrogant! Ought you not rather to mourn? Let him who has done this be removed from among you.

[3] For though absent in body, I am present in spirit; and as if present, I have already pronounced judgment on the one who did such a thing. [4] When you are assembled in the name of the Lord Jesus and my spirit is present, with the power of our Lord Jesus, [5] you are to deliver this man to Satan for the destruction of the flesh, so that his spirit may be saved in the day of the Lord. (vv. 1–5)

6. What are the Corinthians tolerating (v. 1)? What's their attitude toward this person and his sin (v. 2)?

7. What does Paul tell the Corinthians to do about this (v. 2)?

8. When and how, specifically, does Paul tell the church to address this man's sin (vv. 3–5)?

9. Who does Paul hold to be finally accountable for tolerating this man's sin?

In these two passages we see that it is the local church as a whole that is finally responsible for ensuring that sound doctrine is preached and that the lives of church members are in line with the gospel.

This means that all of us have a responsibility for the church's teaching and its members' lives, and all of us will give an account to God for how we've handled this responsibility.

10. If you're accountable in some sense for the godly testimony of the members of your church, how should you respond when:

- Someone sins against you? Does it matter how serious the sin is?
- You come to learn about a serious sin in someone's life?

11. As we saw in Galatians 1, every church member is accountable to ensure that their church preaches the gospel faithfully. What are some practical ways you can exercise this responsibility? (Hint: Consider Acts 17:11 as a starting point.)

FOR FURTHER STUDY:

To learn more about the whole congregation's responsibility for its membership, discipline, and doctrine, consider:

- Matthew 18:15–17
- 2 Corinthians 2:6
- 2 Timothy 4:3

TEACHER'S NOTES FOR WEEK 1

DIGGING IN

1. In this passage, Nebuchadnezzar says that God's kingdom and dominion are everlasting and that his rule is over all the inhabitants of heaven and earth.

2. Nebuchadnezzar says that God does whatever he pleases among the inhabitants of his earth, and none can hinder his plans or question their justice. In other words, God exercises complete sovereignty and authority over human beings.

3. Answers will vary. A Christian's heart should rejoice and be humbled and offer worship when we contemplate God's unrivaled sovereignty over everything. But too often pride wells up within us and we think, "That's not fair!" But to rebel in our hearts against God's rule is the very essence of sin. So we must cultivate appropriate reverence, awe, and humility before God, rejoicing that he is the King of all and we are his subjects.

4. Man is created in *God's* image (v. 26).

5. That man is created in God's image means that he is to exercise dominion over the creation, righteously stewarding its resources and imaging God's rule over it (vv. 26, 28). Thus, in verse 28 God tells the first man and woman to be fruitful and multiply, to fill the earth and subdue it.

6. From this passage we learn that God has delegated a measure of authority over creation to all human beings. Further, we learn that exercising authority over creation is part of what it means to be human. Since all of us are made in the image of God, all of us are to righteously exercise authority over creation.

7. Romans 13:1–7 speaks of the authority God grants to the government. He grants this authority for the purpose of rewarding those who do good and punishing those who do evil in order to promote the good of society (Rom. 13:4; see also 1 Pet. 2:13–17). He also grants the authority to levy taxes! Therefore, in response, we are to honor, submit to, obey, and pay taxes to our governing authorities (Rom. 13:7).

Ephesians 6:1–4 speaks to the authority God has given to parents over their children. He grants them authority to teach, train, and discipline their children so as to teach them how to live according to God's will (see also Heb. 12:5–11). Children, who are under this authority, are to respond by submitting to and obeying their parents.

Hebrews 13:7, 17 speaks to the authority God has given to leaders in the church. This authority is for the purpose of teaching God's Word, leading the church, and modeling a godly way of life in order that the church would grow to maturity in Christ. In response, church members are to submit to their leaders and imitate their way of life insofar as the church's leaders follow Christ (see 1 Cor. 11:1).

8. Righteousness and the fear of God are what characterize the exercise of authority David describes in verse 3.

9. Answers will vary, but the basic idea is that in order for any person to rightly exercise authority, we must recognize that we are *under* God's authority. If we recognize that we are under God's authority we will submit to his will. We will strive to wield authority righteously and for others' good, just as God does to us. We will recognize that our will isn't absolute—only God's is. If we *don't* exercise authority in the fear of God, we will be tempted to rule over others harshly, to abuse authority for our own benefit and others' hurt, and to take advantage of those under us rather than using our authority to bless them.

10. According to David, when someone rules righteously over men, the effect is like the sun shining ever more brightly until it reaches full noon, and like rain that waters the earth. This twin imagery speaks to godly authority as something that brings life, vitality, and growth to those who are under it. Personal experiences of this will vary, but hopefully participants will be able to recall positive experiences of parents, teachers, church leaders, government leaders, and others exercising authority in a godly and righteous way.

11. In light of all these passages, an appropriate response would be something like, "Of course authority can be abused, and when it is, that's an awful thing. God clearly condemns that in his Word. But the right use of authority reflects the character of God himself. He is Lord and he rules over all the universe. And he created us in his image, to exercise authority over creation. Further, he gives specific kinds of authority to the government, to parents, to employers, and to leaders in the church. This authority is meant to bless, protect, help, and build up others, and is to be exercised in the fear of God and in submission to his will."

12. Answers will vary.

TEACHER'S NOTES FOR WEEK 2

DIGGING IN

1. According to this passage, the shepherds of Israel have fed themselves and clothed themselves while neglecting the sheep (vv. 2–3). Verse 4 tells us that they haven't strengthened the weak, healed the sick, bound up the injured, brought back the strayed, or sought out the lost.

In other words, they've made themselves wealthy by exploiting the poor among Israel rather than doing justice. Further, by living unrighteously, they've abdicated their spiritual responsibility to lead the people in obeying God. Thus, this passage likely refers to concrete acts of economic exploitation which the leaders of Israel perpetrated against the nation.

2. As a result of the shepherds' unrighteousness and negligence, God's people were scattered over all the face of the earth, becoming food for the wild beasts (vv. 5–6). This is referring to the exile, in which, as an act of judgment for the people's—and especially the leaders'—sin, God caused his people to be taken captive by a foreign nation.

3. God's attitude toward the shepherds is one of righteous indignation. He promises to judge the shepherds, to put a stop to their evil actions, and to rescue his people from them (vv. 7–10).

4. In verses 11–16, God promises to:

- Search for his sheep and seek them out among all the places they've been scattered (vv. 11–12);
- Bring them out from the countries to which they've been scattered, and bring them into their own land (v. 13);
- Feed them with good pasture (vv. 13–14);
- Cause them to lie down in safety (v. 14);
- Shepherd them himself (v. 15);
- Seek the lost (v. 16);
- Bring back the strayed (v. 16);
- Bind up the injured (v. 16);
- Strengthen the weak (v. 16);
- Destroy the fat and strong who have oppressed the flock (v. 16).

In other words, God promises to personally care for his people, undoing the harm that the unrighteous shepherds have done and securing their total well-being.

5. God's promise to gather and feed his sheep (vv. 11–14) reveals that he is a God who provides for his people and that he cares for all of their needs.

6. God's promise to seek the lost, bring back the strayed, and strengthen the weak (v. 16) reveals that he is compassionate and tender. God pities his people's weaknesses and personally condescends to care for them.

7. God's promise to destroy those who had abused his people and to shepherd his people in justice (v. 16) reveals that he is holy and just. God will punish those who harm, exploit, and abuse others, and his rule over his people is perfectly righteous toward all.

8. That God is the shepherd of his people means that we should:

- Depend on him to supply all our needs (Ps. 23:1–3).
- Expectantly trust that he will care for us in all circumstances (Ps. 23:4).
- Humbly submit to his discipline and correction (Ps. 23:4).
- Offer him joyful worship and praise (Ps. 95:6–7).

9. God promises that when he rescues his flock, he will set up his servant David over them to shepherd them (vv. 22–24).

10. God fulfills this promise by sending Jesus, the son of David and the Good Shepherd, to reign over his people and shepherd them in righteousness forever (Jer. 23:5–6; Luke 1:32–33; John 10:11–18).

11. The prophecy of Jeremiah 3:15, that God will establish *shepherds* after his own heart, leads us to expect that he will lead his people not merely by his one Chief Shepherd (cf. 1 Pet. 5:4) but by many other righteous shepherds under his authority.

This prophecy is fulfilled in the church as Christ gives the gifts of pastors (or elders) to his church (Eph. 4:8–12), who lead them, teach them to understand God's Word (Jer. 3:15), and shepherd them according to God's will (1 Pet. 5:3).

12. All of these passages, taken together, teach us that pastors are to:

- Lead the church righteously, imitating God's own character (Jer. 3:15).
- Feed God's people what they need, which is God's Word (Jer. 3:15; John 21:15–17; 2 Tim. 4:2).
- Not exploit God's people for selfish gain but instead be examples to the flock (Ezek. 34:1–6; 1 Pet. 5:2).
- Give special care for members of the flock who are weak or ill (Ezek. 34:16; James 5:14), especially those who are spiritually weak or ill.

- Pursue those who wander from the flock (Ezek. 34:16), exercising loving discipline that mirrors the way God handles us when we stray.

13. Answers will vary. The basic idea is that by giving us a rich picture of the character of God and the way *he* exercises authority, these passages show us what God expects from those in authority. And what he expects is nothing less than shepherding the way *he* does. This means that the abuse of authority is *never* God's will, and those who claim divine sanction for abusing authority are only showing that they don't deserve to wield that authority in the first place. This should comfort and encourage those who are skeptical of authority—and should undermine that skepticism!—because the authority God wants to see is an authority that reflects his own character, an authority that is righteous, compassionate, loving, and self-sacrificing for the good of others.

14. Answers will vary.

TEACHER'S NOTES FOR WEEK 3

DIGGING IN

1. In verse 1, Peter appeals to the elders on the basis of:

- his status as a fellow elder;
- his role as a witness of the sufferings of Christ;
- and his share in the glory that is to come, just as these elders do.

Peter likely mentions these things in order to remind these elders of his authority (as an eyewitness of Christ), his sympathy with their struggles (as a fellow elder), and of the hope of an eternal reward which awaits those who serve Christ faithfully.

2. The main command Peter gives to the elders in v. 2 is that they are to shepherd the flock of God. Everything that follows describes the manner in which they are (or are not!) to shepherd the church.

3. Practically speaking, to shepherd a church means:

- to faithfully feed the church God's Word by teaching it regularly (John 21:15–17);
- to protect the church from false teachers through careful teaching and discipline;
- to lead the church as a whole in ways that are faithful to God's Word;
- and to attend to the state of each church member's soul, caring for spiritual needs, helping to bear burdens, and leading each member to greater conformity to Christ.

4. The completed chart should look something like this:

Don't Shepherd Like This. . . .	Instead, Shepherd Like *This*. . . .
As though under compulsion (v. 2)	Exercising oversight (v. 2)
For shameful (that is, selfish monetary) gain (v. 2)	Willingly (v. 2)
Domineering over those in your charge (v. 3)	As God would have you (v. 2)
	Eagerly (v. 2)
	Being examples to the flock (v.3)

Answers to the discussion questions will vary.

5. Peter says that when Jesus comes back, faithful elders will receive the unfading crown of glory (v. 4).

This should this encourage elders because through all the hardships they endure for Christ's sake now, they look forward to the enjoyment of an eternal reward.

This should humble them because God's reward of their labors is a gracious gift they do not deserve. Further, Peter refers to Christ as the Chief Shepherd, which reminds the elders that they are merely undershepherds who are accountable to their Lord.

6. Peter tells the rest of the church to submit to the elders (v. 5). This requires humility because submission is a posture of being willing to follow and obey someone else's leadership and teaching. None of us like to submit to others by nature. We all must cultivate humility in order to obey God by following our church's leaders.

7. Paul so extensively discusses his own way of life and teaching in this address to the Ephesian elders because he is holding himself up as an example for them to follow. In his personal conduct, his teaching, and his pastoral work, Paul established himself as a model for the Ephesian elders to follow. Now, when he has one last chance to speak to them, he is reminding them of his own example so that they will follow it in their own ministries.

8. Paul's way of life among the Ephesians was characterized by:

- serving the Lord with all humility and with tears (v. 19);
- declaring to them everything that was profitable (v. 20), teaching in public and in people's homes (v. 20);
- testifying to Jews and Greeks that they should repent and believe in Christ (v. 21),
- declaring the whole counsel of God (v. 27);
- day and night admonishing everyone with tears (v. 31);
- not coveting anyone's possessions (v. 33);
- working to support himself and provide for others so that he might be an example of Jesus's saying that it is more blessed to give than to receive (vv. 34–35).

9. Paul's example is a vivid fulfillment and example of the things Peter says should characterize elders. As an apostle and church planter, Paul established the example that the elders in Ephesus were to follow. As such,

- he set an example of godliness for all the Christians to follow (1 Pet. 5:3);

- he diligently shepherded the flock at Ephesus (1 Pet. 5:2);
- he did so willingly, not under compulsion, and clearly not for selfish gain, since he coveted no one's money (1 Pet. 5:2–3);
- clearly he did not domineer over those under his charge (1 Pet 5:3), but instead lovingly taught, cared for, exhorted, and set an example for them.

10. Paul charges the Ephesian elders to:

- pay careful attention to themselves and to all the flock (v. 28);
- to care for (literally "shepherd") the flock (v. 28);
- to be alert against false teachers (v. 31);
- to help the weak (v. 35).

By implication, Paul also exhorts them to follow everything he did in his ministry, proclaiming the whole counsel of God, calling people to repent and believe, and personally ministering the gospel to everyone in their charge.

11. Answers will vary. Hopefully, people will recognize that serving as an elder is a difficult and demanding task, since they are required to faithfully teach, shepherd, protect against false teachers, and set an example of godliness for the whole church.

12–13. Answers will vary.

TEACHER'S NOTES FOR WEEK 4

DIGGING IN

1. According to this passage, an elder must be:

   1) above reproach (v. 2);

   2) the husband of one wife (v. 2);

   3) sober-minded (v. 2);

   4) self-controlled (v. 2);

   5) respectable (v. 2);

   6) hospitable (v. 2);

   7) able to teach (v. 2);

   8) not a drunkard (v. 3);

   9) not violent but gentle (v. 3);

   10) not quarrelsome (v. 3);

   11) not a lover of money (v. 3);

   12) a good manager of his household, keeping his children submissive (vv. 4–5);

   13) not a recent convert (v. 6);

   14) well thought of by outsiders (v. 7).

2. To be "above reproach" (v. 2) is to have a consistently godly character that is not open to the charge of living in any serious, overt sin. "Above reproach" doesn't mean perfect. All Christians still struggle with sin (James 3:1–2). But to be an elder, a man must have a consistently, thoroughly godly character.

3. The qualification "husband of one wife," literally "one-woman man," means that a married man must be completely faithful to his wife. It doesn't seem that this verse *requires* that a man be married (after all, Paul commends singleness for the purpose of ministry in 1 Corinthians 7). Rather, since the vast majority of men marry, this verse simply assumes that and asserts that an elder must be sexually faithful. Obviously, a single man who would be an elder must have sexual integrity as well.

4. Answers will vary.

5. Hospitality is a qualification for being an elder because it demonstrates generous care for others (v. 2). Christian hospitality should consist of welcoming fellow Christians into one's home, especially Christians who are in

need. It should involve providing for fellow Christians' material needs as well as encouraging them spiritually.

6. According to Titus 1:9–10, it is important for elders to be able to teach so that they are able to instruct the church in the truth and refute those who teach false doctrine.

7. In 1 Timothy 2:12, Paul writes, "I do not permit a woman to teach or to exercise authority over a man." And he grounds this command not in a cultural custom or temporary circumstance, but in creation itself, indicating that this is a normative, ongoing teaching for all churches to follow. In light of the fact that authoritative teaching is a key responsibility of elders, this means that Scripture does not permit women to serve as elders. Rather, only qualified men should fill that role.

8. What the qualifications listed in verse 3 ("not a drunkard, not violent but gentle, not quarrelsome, not a lover of money") have in common is that they all refer to self-control, to mastery of appetites. A man who isn't a drunkard controls his use of alcohol. A man who is "not violent but gentle" controls his desire for revenge or honor and instead humbles himself to serve someone else in love. And a man who is not a lover of money has mastered the desire for material things. He's come to treat money and possessions as God's gifts entrusted to him so that he would use them faithfully rather than coveting them and hoarding them.

9. Paul insists that a man must manage his household well in order to be an elder (vv. 4–5) because a man's home life is one of the truest tests of his character. A man lives with his wife and children every day. And he is responsible before God to lead them spiritually. Whether a man's children obey him is a test of how well he teaches them, disciplines them, and models godly living for them. Thus, if a man is a godly leader, it will be evident in his home life. And if he's not, it will be evident in his home life. That's why Paul says, "If someone does not know how to manage his own household, how will he care for God's church?" (v. 5).

10. A recent convert would be susceptible to becoming puffed up with conceit and falling into the condemnation of the Devil (v. 6) because he has not developed the kind of tested character that comes through faithfully following Jesus over a long time. If a new convert is put in a position of prominence as an elder, he's likely to let the privilege go to his head. He may be likely to begin to think of himself more highly than he ought to think. And, as Scripture teaches, pride goes before a fall. Thus, an elder must be someone whose character and maturity have been tested and proved through a relatively long course of following Christ.

11. What's at stake in an elder's reputation among non-Christians is the reputation of Christ in the world. All Christians are called to represent Christ to the world and to commend the gospel by their good deeds. All Christians bear the name of Christ. Elders, since they are officially recognized leaders of the church, have a special responsibility and a heightened visibility before the world. The world will look first to the church's leaders to see if they live according to what they teach. If a church's leaders are hypocrites, they discredit the gospel and the church in the eyes of the world.

12. As we discussed in question 9, elders are particularly susceptible to temptation because they are in a position of prominence. This can easily lead to pride and arrogance. Elders can also be tempted to wield their influence harshly (1 Pet. 5:3) or for their own selfish gain (1 Pet. 5:2). And there are many more ways that elders can be tempted.

13–14. Answers will vary.

TEACHER'S NOTES FOR WEEK 5

DIGGING IN

1. The problem the church in Jerusalem faced in this passage is that Hellenistic (Greek-speaking) members of the congregation were complaining against the Hebrew church members because the Greek widows were being overlooked in the daily distribution of food (v. 1).

2. The apostles' solution to the problem was to have the congregation select seven wise and godly men whom the apostles would appoint to take care of the daily distribution of food (vv. 2–4).

3. The apostles told the congregation to pick out men who were of good repute and full of the Holy Spirit and wisdom (v. 3).

4. The reason the apostles gave for delegating this task to another group of men was that they had to devote themselves to the ministry of the Word and prayer, and that it would be wrong for them to neglect that in order to attend to the distribution of food (v. 4).

5. The qualifications for deacons Paul lays down that pertain to character are:

- dignified,
- not double tongued,
- not addicted to much wine,
- not greedy for dishonest gain.

One word that summarizes all of these is "self-control." Another is "integrity." A deacon must be admirable in his conduct, must control his appetites, and must be truthful in his speech.

6. To "hold the mystery of the faith with a clear conscience" means to be sound in both belief and action. To hold the mystery of the faith is to steadfastly believe the good news that God has revealed in Christ. And to do so with a clear conscience means to *not* live in a way that undermines one's claim to follow Christ (1 Tim. 3:9).

7. Paul insists that deacons be tested before they serve because deacons are entrusted with responsibility (v. 10). In addressing some of the church's physical needs, they will be entrusted with material resources, and they will interact with many different members of the church. Thus, they must demonstrate that they are able to handle this responsibility with integrity and diligence before being entrusted with it.

8. In terms of their family life, Paul requires that deacons be faithful to their wives and manage their households well (v. 12).

9. What's present in the qualification for elders in 1 Timothy 3:4–5 that's absent in the qualification for deacons in 3:12 is that for elders, Paul reasons, "For if someone does not know how to manage his own household, how will he care for God's church?" This teaches us that Paul expected elders to care for the church, that is, to lead it, in a similar way to how a husband leads and cares for his family. That Paul doesn't reiterate this argument with respect to deacons seems to indicate that deacons do not have the kind of authoritative leadership role that elders do.

10. Deacons who serve well gain "a good standing for themselves and also great confidence in the faith that is in Christ Jesus" (1 Tim. 3:13). This is because faithfully serving God and his people results in our being commended in God's sight and before the church. Further, faithfully serving God and his people builds up one's confidence in Christ and in the power of the gospel to transform us into his image.

11. The one qualification for elders that's *not* also a qualification for deacons is that elders must be able to teach (1 Tim. 3:2). This tells us that one of the responsibilities of the office of elder is to teach God's Word. On the other hand, it is *not* one of the responsibilities of the office of deacon. That doesn't mean that deacons *can't* teach the Bible. It simply means that it is not one of their responsibilities as deacons. Thus, just as deacons are not charged with overseeing the church as elders are, neither are they required to teach the Word as elders are.

12–13. Answers will vary.

TEACHER'S NOTES FOR WEEK 6

DIGGING IN

1. Paul was astonished that the Galatians were deserting the God who called them in the grace of Christ and were turning to a different gospel, which was really no gospel at all (vv. 6–7).

2. Those who are troubling the Galatians are distorting the gospel of Christ (v. 7).

3. In verses 8 and 9, Paul twice pronounces a curse on anyone who preaches a "gospel" other than the true one. Preaching a false gospel is such a serious matter because all of our eternal destinies hang on our belief in the gospel.

4. Paul's letter is addressed to the churches of Galatia (v. 1). He's not just speaking to the churches' leaders; he's speaking to everyone in the churches!

5. According to this passage, all the members of local churches are ultimately responsible for ensuring that the church is teaching sound doctrine.

6. The Corinthians are tolerating a church member who is having a sexual relationship with his father's wife (v. 1). Their attitude toward this person and his sin is one of arrogant boasting and approval (v. 2).

7. Paul tells the Corinthians to remove this man from their fellowship (v. 2).

8. Specifically, Paul tells them to remove this man from their fellowship *when* they come together as a church. When they are all assembled together, they are to act as a church to remove him from their membership, which is what Paul is getting at when he speaks of handing the man "delivering to Satan" (vv. 3–5).

9. In this passage Paul rebukes the whole church for tolerating this man's sin. Further, he tells the whole church to act in order to remove the man from fellowship. Thus, Paul holds the whole church finally accountable for this moral issue, not only its leaders.

10. Since we are in some sense accountable for the godly testimony of the members of our church, we should consider carefully what we need to do when someone sins against us. If it's something minor, we should probably just pass over it, forgive them, and move on (Prov. 19:11; 1 Pet. 4:8). If the sin is more serious, we should confront them according to Jesus's instructions in Matthew 18:15–17. If the person doesn't respond to our private rebuke, then, in obedience to Jesus's teachings, we should involve others in the church.

If you come to learn about a serious sin in someone else's life, you have a responsibility to do something about it. If you know the person well, it may be wise to privately, personally confront him or her. If you don't know the person well, you may want to talk to one of your church's elders or pastors about it. Be wary of the temptation to gossip, but asking a church leader to help address a serious sin in someone's life is not gossip. It's seeking to turn a sinner from the error of his or her way in order to save that person from death and cover over a multitude of sins (James 5:19–20).

11. Here are some ways you could faithfully exercise your responsibility to ensure that your church's preaching is faithful to the gospel:

- Regularly pray for your pastor and others who teach in your church. Pray that all of their teaching would be faithful to God's Word.
- Study Scripture on your own, so that you will be better able to discern error when it comes across your path.
- Pray that God would give you a humble, gracious spirit *and* the courage to confront error when that may be necessary.
- If you hear something from a teacher in your church that seems wrong, ask a trusted, mature Christian who knows the Bible well what they thought about it, or ask the teacher for clarification. Assume that he is in the right and that you simply misunderstood. Patiently listen to his explanation. And if you become convinced that your teacher has taught error, approach another leader in the church to let him know your concern.

PERSONAL NOTES

PERSONAL NOTES

PERSONAL NOTES

PERSONAL NOTES

PERSONAL NOTES

PERSONAL NOTES

Building Healthy Churches

9Marks exists to equip church leaders with a biblical vision and practical resources for displaying God's glory to the nations through healthy churches.

To that end, we want to see churches characterized by these nine marks of health:

1   Expositional Preaching
2   Biblical Theology
3   A Biblical Understanding of the Gospel
4   A Biblical Understanding of Conversion
5   A Biblical Understanding of Evangelism
6   Biblical Church Membership
7   Biblical Church Discipline
8   Biblical Discipleship
9   Biblical Church Leadership

Find all our Crossway titles
and other resources at
www.9Marks.org

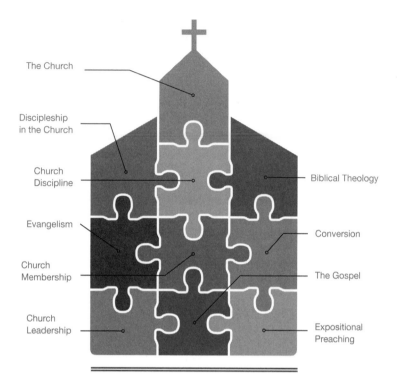

The Church

Discipleship
in the Church

Church
Discipline

Evangelism

Church
Membership

Church
Leadership

Biblical Theology

Conversion

The Gospel

Expositional
Preaching

Be sure to check out the rest of the
**9MARKS HEALTHY CHURCH
STUDY GUIDE SERIES**

This series covers the nine distinctives
of a healthy church as originally laid out
in *Nine Marks of a Healthy Church* by
Mark Dever. Each book explores the
biblical foundations of key aspects of
the church, helping Christians to live
out those realities as members of a
local body. A perfect resource for use in
Sunday school, church-wide studies, or
small group contexts.